Cultivating a Life of Joy:
IN 8 SIMPLE WAYS

Tricia Lovvorn Patterson

Copyright © 2017 Tricia Patterson

All rights reserved.

ISBN: 1975815653
ISBN-13: 978-1975815653

DEDICATION

To my daughter, Joy.

Every time I say your name, I'm reminded of the sweet gift of joy that our Savior alone brings.
As your mother, I'm constantly reminded of my deep need for Jesus every single day. I am refined, refilled, and renewed daily as Jesus makes me more like Him.

I pray that my life will reflect the joy that Jesus alone brings, so that you can learn what it truly means to cultivate a life of joy through the intimate relationship with our loving God.

CONTENTS

	A Note From Tricia	i
1	Realism + Hope > Optimism	10
2	Dependence + Trust > Independence + Control	15
3	A Daily Filling of the Spirit	20
4	Grumbling + Complaining Deplete Joy	25
5	Isolation Breeds Self-Pity	30
6	Self-pity Extinguishes the Flame of Joy	37
7	Productivity + Purpose > Laziness + Misplaced Priorities	42
8	Unconfessed Sin = The Greatest Thief of Joy	47

A NOTE FROM TRICIA

We all desire to live a life marked by joy, but the circumstances of life can trip us up and get us off course at times.

Let me share with you 8 simple ways to cultivate the attitude of joy in your life

Dear friend,

First off, I am so PUMPED that you chose to read this simple guide to cultivating a life of joy! There is a big difference between circumstantial-happiness and the life-lasting joy that is available through Jesus Christ. I am currently entering a season that is not necessarily conducive to circumstantial-happiness. So, I completely understand if you're in a place in your life that is bringing you down. I'm there too. I'm in the midst of a major transition in my life. My husband is starting a new job where he will be traveling a lot, we're moving from the place where we've built our lives for the past 10 years, and life feels very uncertain, scary, and lonely at times. So, I get it!

When I polled my friends about what devotional they'd like for me to write, the overwhelming majority said "CULTIVATING A LIFE OF JOY!" Immediately after this clear call to write on cultivating joy, I entered into an emotional state that was *very joy-less*. I thought, "WHO AM I TO WRITE ON JOY?" And, that's where the Lord began teaching me. He showed me that these truths I'm about to share with you will be my *lifelines* throughout this next season in my life. I am walking this road with you. I am not *feeling* joyful, but I am *choosing* joy.

I have learned throughout the years that joy is 100% a choice. It is not a personality trait. It is not an emotion. It is a choice of attitude. Even when joy doesn't make sense, we *choose* to rejoice in the Lord. We do not rejoice in our circumstances, because sometimes our circumstances are just *not joy-worthy*. We rejoice in our Lord in the midst of difficulties, in the midst of struggles, in the midst of pain, because it's in those moments that others see God working in and through us. Why choose joy? Because by choosing joy, we point to God's power in our lives. By choosing joy, we choose to glorify God. By choosing joy, we shine a light in this dark world. By choosing joy, we proclaim the overwhelming victory we have in Christ.

THAT is why choosing joy is worth it. So let me give you 8 simple ways to cultivate joy in your life.

Love,

Tricia

DAY 1
Realism + Hope > Optimism

Yep, you read that right! The combination of realism + hope creates a much healthier perspective than fickle, unrealistic, unreliable optimism. People who know me may be surprised by this statement. For many years, I likely would have been labeled as a mindless optimist. (Very Sue Heck-esque…*The Middle* anyone?) Now, don't get me wrong, there is nothing wrong with optimism, and optimism in its truest sense is very biblical. But, when life gets difficult…when your husband leaves you after years of marriage, when your child is diagnosed with a terminal disease, when your friends reject you, when you've been dumped, when you feel deflated and defeated by life, optimism doesn't seem like a realistic option.

The reality of living in a broken and fallen world is that life here on earth will not always be easy. Life here on earth may bring troubles and sadness and pain. BUT, because of Christ's work on the Cross and because of His resurrection, we possess a LIVING HOPE. Jesus was very upfront about the reality of difficulty that could come while on this earth. He tells us in John 16:33, "Here on earth you will have many trials and sorrows." *Realism*. We *will* have trials and sorrows, but let's read the entire the verse.

"I have told you all this so that you may have *peace* in me. Here on earth you will have many trials and sorrows. But *take heart*, because I have *overcome* the world." *Hope.* Jesus has overcome this world. In the words of Ellie Holcomb:

> *We've got this hope*
> *We've got a future*
> *We've got the power of the resurrection living within*
> *We've got this hope*
> *We've got a promise*
> *That we are held up and protected in the palm of His hand*
>
> *And even when our hearts are breaking*
> *Even when our souls are shaken*
> *Ohhh, we've got this hope*
> *Even when the tears are falling*
> *Even when the night is calling*
> *Ohhh, we've got this hope*
>
> *And we're not alone*
> *Our God is with us*
> *We can approach the throne with confidence 'cause He made a way*
> *When trouble comes*
> *He'll be our fortress*
> *We know that those who place their hope in Him will not be ashamed*
>
> *Our hope is grounded in an empty grave*
> *Our hope is founded on the promises that He made*

Her words are the perfect picture of the marriage between realism and hope. We can approach life with joy because we hold on to a hope that is living and real. We hold on to the expectation of our future with Jesus. We have the confidence of His presence with us every step of the way on this earth. We can trust in Him even when life is unsettling, because He has more in store for us than we can possibly imagine. The living hope He promises us sustains our peace and joy. The living hope we have is the *anchor* for our joy. The reality of the future that is ahead of us allows us to live a life marked by an eternal perspective, which takes us over the mountains of our struggles & trials in this life and lifts us up to a place of joy.

> *"I pray that God, the source of hope, will fill you completely with joy and peace because you trust in him. Then you will overflow with confident hope through the power of the Holy Spirit." (Romans 15:13)*

DIVING DEEPER

Read:
Hebrews 6:17-20

How would you describe the hope that we have to hold on to as the anchor of our souls?

_____

_____

_____

_____

How do the promises of God act as an anchor in your life?

_____

_____

_____

_____

PERSONAL REFLECTION

What circumstances in your life are leaving you confused, unsettled, and flailing rather than secure, firm, and anchored?

_____

_____

_____

_____

What promise of God are you going to hold firmly to as the anchor for your soul right now?

_____

_____

_____

_____

CHALLENGE

Write down one promise of God. As you go about your day, remind yourself of that solid promise when you feel yourself wavering as the storms of life hit.

_____

_____

DAY 2
Dependence + Trust > Independence + Control

Just as Romans 15:13 says: You will be filled completely with joy and peace **because** you trust in Him. Dependence and trust in God are the means by which you receive joy and peace. Are there any other control freaks out there? This desire for control and independence can be paralyzing in our lives. This desire for control over our lives leaves us depleted of joy. Why? Because the lack of trust in God robs us of the joyous experience of letting go and experiencing the ride of life that comes from depending on Jesus. Trusting God's sovereignty & control over the circumstances of your life brings true joy.

I remember a time in my life where I was very lacking in joy and very full of anxiety. The central issue: lack of trust in God. After Sam and I got married, I went through a time that I dealt with a great amount of anxiety. Rewind about 7 years ago. I was in a constant state of fear, panic, and anxiety. I had just graduated from college, gotten married the weekend after, came home from the honeymoon to move into an apartment, moved from that apartment to a new house because of very terrible circumstances at the apartment, I was looking for a job, got a job that was very much outside of my training and desires, started graduate school, and felt very isolated in my new life as a married-woman while all my friends were still in college down the road.

So, here I was newly married, with a patient & understanding husband, yet I was in this constant state of fear, worry, and panic. Sam travels some for work, and that's when the panic and worry would set in even more. When he was out of town, I was filled with every irrational fear that is possible. I lived with a mind constantly swirling in the "what-if" world. *What-if his plane goes down. What-if someone knows I'm home alone. What-if I pass out and no one knows. What-if something happens to me, what if something happens to him. What-if, what-if, what-if.* There were times that my heart rate would hit the 200s because I was in this state of panic. I panicked about my panic. We even went to the hospital one time because of chest pains. They couldn't figure out why my heart rate was so high. The doctor told me that he could prescribe anxiety medicine for me, but he wanted to be cautious. He explained that by assuming anxiety was the problem, that every other doctor in the future would merely assent many other problems to anxiety. It was that conversation with that doctor that opened my eyes to this major issue going on deep within my soul. Why was I so plagued by anxiety? This was a deep rooted issue that I needed to deal with.

One morning, Sam was about to go out of town. I was laying next to him that morning and the fears and worries started trickling in. I was holding on to him and remember saying to God, *"You can't let anything happen to him. He's mine."* Clear as day, the Lord said: "Tricia, that's where you're wrong. He's not **yours**. He's **mine**." I'll never forget that conversation with the Lord, because it changed my life forever. I had been clinging to everything in my life as if it was mine. That morning, the Lord got in my face in a way to awaken me to the truth I always knew, but wasn't willing to accept. This is not *my* life. This is not *my* husband.

None of this is *mine*. I am not in control. Everything I have is a gift He's given me. The breath I take. Every beat of my heart. It's all His. He brought this verse to my mind, which has been a theme of my life: "If you cling to your life you will lose it, but if you give up your life for me, you will find true life." (Matthew 10:39) That day, the Lord started the process of teaching me the art of *"loose-grip living"*. He had to pry my fingers off of my life to get me to this point. I now seek to hold everything in my life with a loose-grip: my family, my husband, my daughter, my future, my dreams, my goals. Because I'm reminded...it is all his anyway. He's the one in control. And, I can trust Him because He is trustworthy.

If you want to cultivate a life of joy, first you must cultivate a life of trust & dependence. Otherwise, you'll be gripping to control so tightly that you'll choke every bit of joy out of your life.

DIVING DEEPER

Read:
Jeremiah 17:5-10

Describe the difference between the person whose "trust is in man" and the person whose "trust is in the Lord."

_____

_____

_____

_____

PERSONAL REFLECTION

Which type of person are you? The one who trusts in man? Or the one who trusts in God?

_____

_____

_____

_____

What do you need to surrender to God today? What are you trying to control, rather than trusting God and letting Him take control?

_____

_____

_____

_____

CHALLENGE

Allow God to search and examine your heart as vs. 10 says.

DAY 3
A Daily Filling of the Spirit

Let's get back to Romans 15:13: *"I pray that God, the source of hope, will fill you completely with joy and peace because you trust in him. Then you will overflow with confident hope through the power of the Holy Spirit."*

"Through the power of the Holy Spirit" — Even with the greatest amount of willpower we can muster up, we cannot accomplish this life marked by hope, trust, peace, and joy apart from the work of the Holy Spirit in our lives. Willpower is so overrated. Willpower will leave you burnt out. Tired. Weary. Exhausted. Undone. But, the power of the Living God? Wow. When you are at your weakest, He has the power to storm in and shower your soul with peace, rest, joy, and hope. I am such a weak person, y'all. My flesh fails me often. Psalm 73:26: "My flesh and my heart may fail, but God is the strength of my heart and my portion forever." Thank God, that He is my strength and my portion! Because I am in **great** need of Him every single day. Are you desperate for God's filling (and refilling) every day? I'm convinced that desperation is a gift from God. I cannot hold life together all on my own. I cannot hold myself together all on my own. I desperately need a fuel and refuel of His Spirit every day. Every single hour. Every single minute. Every single moment.

Let's talk theology for a second. When we accept Jesus Christ as our Lord and Savior, we are instantly indwelled by the Holy Spirit. He takes up residence in our lives. He never leaves us. We can never lose Him.

BUT, we do choose to tap into His power on a daily basis. I can live my daily life through my own strength, or I can choose to tap into the power of God living within my soul. Some days I choose self. Other days, I choose the Spirit. The days I choose the Spirit are MUCH BETTER. Much more joy-filled. I heard this explained by a pastor at our church once. He said that each believer has this pilot light of the Spirit within our souls. Some of us leave it as just that. The Holy Spirit sits there waiting to be ignited, but we never fan into flames the work of the Spirit in our lives. (2 Timothy 1:6 "I remind you to fan into flame the gift of God.") Instead of quenching the work of the Holy Spirit in our lives, may we daily fan into flames the gift of God!

How do we fan into flames the fire of the Spirit in our lives?

1. Bring yourself before the presence of God daily.
I seek to live by the simple words of the song, *In the Morning When I Rise:*

In the morning when I rise, In the morning when I rise, In the morning when I rise,

Give me Jesus, Give me Jesus, Give me Jesus
You can have all this world, But give me Jesus

When we intentionally bring ourselves before the presence of God in dependence, we make room for the Lord to come in and work.

Practical ways for coming before His presence:
- Starting your day with worship music.
- Starting your day by journaling prayers and thoughts to God.
- Starting your day by reading the Bible.

2. Acknowledge your need for Him.
By simply acknowledging our need for God in our daily lives we open ourselves up to His working power in our daily lives.

3. Explicitly ask Him to fill you with His Spirit.
Sounds simple right? Well, there is power in verbally asking God to fill us with His Spirit. I try to make this a daily prayer of mine. "Heavenly Father, fill me with your Spirit. Less of me, and more of you."

CULTIVATING A LIFE OF JOY

DIVING DEEPER

Read:
John 15:1-11

Ephesians 5:18 says: *"Do not get drunk on wine, which leads to debauchery. Instead, be filled with the Spirit."*
The original Greek word for "be filled" means to "keep on being filled constantly and continually."

After reading John 15:1-11, what characterizes the life of a Christian who is "being filled" constantly and continually?

_____

_____

_____

_____

PERSONAL REFLECTION

When we are depleted of the Spirit's filling in our lives, we often react out of our flesh & sinful nature, rather than the Spirit's leading. What are some of your most common "reactive responses" when you aren't being filled & led by the Spirit?
I'll start: Irritability, frustration, impatience, anxiety. You?

_____

_____

_____

_____

What action steps are you going to take to get in the presence of God daily (to abide in Christ), so that you can continually be filled with His Spirit?

_____

_____

_____

_____

CHALLENGE

Choose a time & place where you will spend time alone with God, every single day for the next week.

DAY 4
Grumbling + Complaining Deplete Joy

"Do everything without complaining and grumbling, so that no one can criticize you. Live clean, innocent lives as children of God, shining like bright lights in a world full of crooked and perverse people." (Philippians 2:14-15)

You guys, sometimes I find myself being such a grumbler and complainer. I mentioned our new life transition with my husband's new job and our move to a new city… As this transition began, my constant grumbling commenced, as well. To be fair, we did have a variety of very annoying circumstances come all at once in our new city which included a stolen wallet, inability to fly home because of the stolen driver's license, an additional 6-hour road trip home with a toddler, a hotel shower that clogged and filled to our knees in 2.5 seconds, a delayed closing on our new home, a toddler's mad tantrums (for no reason whatsoever), a broken AC when we arrived home, and more… Instead of taking these annoyances in stride, I allowed them to completely deplete my joy. I began complaining and grumbling about *anything and everything*. I began expecting the worst. This heart full of grumbles drained me. My countenance showed it. My body felt it. Grumbles and complaints drain you of all joy.

Now, don't hear me wrong. I completely understand the need to vent. I'm actually a proponent of venting. I think we all need those two or three safe people in our lives who we can share our worst days with. I'm an external processor, so if I don't vent, my head will explode off of my body. But, here's the difference in venting and grumbling: venting releases and expresses frustrations and emotions once, and then leaves the complaints behind. A venting session provides the outlet, then allows you to move forward. Grumbling festers. Complaining brews and stews in our hearts until we're completely saturated by the muck of our laments. A spirit filled with grumbling and complaining is very contrary to a spirit filled with the Living God. Grumbling and complaining quench the work of the Spirit in our lives.

When you find yourself getting caught up in a web of complaints, stop yourself. Hold your tongue. Replace your complaints with thankfulness. Trust me, this is WAY easier said than done. When I was stuck in this web of complaints, I literally **hated** when well-meaning people told me all the things I should be thankful for. I was so annoyed by the thought of being thankful, when I would rather just grumble. But, the reality is that grumbling didn't get me anywhere. It just left me stuck in a grimy place of bitterness and resentment.

Thankfulness, on the other hand, served as a catalyst for my depleted joy. Even when I wasn't *feeling* it, I *forced* myself to think of things to be thankful for. This decision to practice gratefulness actually changed my daily life. I felt better physically, emotionally, and spiritually. If you are feeling depleted in the area of joy, examine your heart. Are you full of gratefulness? Or are you full of grumbles? If you find yourself in a routine of grumbling (because, trust me, I can wire myself into default complaint-mode), turn it around. Start a new routine. Replace your grumbles with gratefulness.

Here's a practical way to apply this: Take out your journal today. Write out 3 things that you're thankful for. Praise God for those 3 things. Tomorrow, write down 3 new things to be thankful for. Praise God. Repeat. Repeat. Repeat. You'll find yourself being lifted above the fog of your complaints and into the sunlight of God's goodness.

I have this reminder on the lock screen of my phone right now (because I need it daily):

"THE ATTITUDE OF JOY STEMS FROM THE ACTION OF THANKFULNESS."

DIVING DEEPER

Read:
1 Thessalonians 5:16-18

Paul gives 3 straightforward commands that we are to follow in order to live in God's will. What are these 3 commands?

_____

_____

_____

_____

PERSONAL REFLECTION

Paul does not say to be thankful "FOR" all circumstances, but he says to be thankful "IN" all circumstances. What can you thank God for in the midst of difficult circumstances?

_____

_____

_____

_____

CHALLENGE

Journal 3 things daily, that you are thankful for. When you find yourself complaining or grumbling, replace the negativity with thankfulness.

DAY 5
Isolation Breeds Self-Pity

We were not meant to live in isolation. God did not make us to live alone. That's why the body of Christ was created. The fellowship of believers is ordained by God for our good and for the advancement of the Kingdom. When we live in isolation, we set ourselves up for self-pity, loneliness, and purposelessness.

Isolation leads you down a dark road towards self-pity. Whereas, fellowship leads you down an illuminated path towards encouragement, comfort, and common purpose.

For some of you, you've *chosen* this place of isolation. You have pulled yourself away from others for one reason or another. Maybe because of insecurity. Maybe because of your fear of failure. Maybe because of your fear of rejection. Maybe you've been hurt in the past, and you don't want to endure that again. Whatever the reason, don't allow it to pull you away from the family that God has intended for you.

We all *long* to *belong*. God desires for you to *know* that you belong. Please hear me, you are loved. You are cared for. You are worthy to be a part of the family of God. Why? Because God has made you worthy. There is no partiality with God. No favoritism. He loves us all the same, and we are to emulate that kind of love in the family of believers. I am truly sorry if someone has caused you pain in the past, and I am praying with you that you will find a fellowship with other believers soon. God is faithful to provide that for us. Go look for it. I bet the fellowship you're longing for is just waiting around the corner.

For some of you, you haven't chosen this place of isolation at all. You've been forced into it. Maybe, like me, you've moved to a new city where you don't know a soul. Or, maybe you're a new mom sitting in a lonely, quiet house with a newborn. Maybe your spouse just left you. Maybe your friends have kicked you out of their group. You've been forced into isolation, and you're longing to get out. I understand. I've been there. I am there. I recently wrote this about my feeling of isolation:

I'm sitting in my new house in my new town, and I feel very isolated and very alone. This house feels empty and so does my soul. I'm not writing these words as part of a pity party. I don't write these words in hopes of your sympathy. I write these words because I know that although I feel alone, I know that I am not alone in this lonely feeling. I know that many, many others feel, have felt, or will feel this at some point. This loneliness that makes your heart sink. That feeling of isolation that makes you feel as though the wind has been knocked out of you. It's painful. It hurts deep. It's reality. But, I keep reminding myself that this feeling, although very real at this moment, is only temporary.

I also find deep comfort in knowing that I'm not alone in this feeling of loneliness. Not that I wish the pain of loneliness on anyone else, but I know that it's the reality for many. I remember a friend talking about the peace and comfort we find in recognizing that we are all part of a fellowship of brokenness. We find solace in this acknowledgment. I'm acknowledging the fellowship of loneliness right now and remembering that I'm not isolated in this feeling. There are many who join me in this place. Come sit at the table with me. No judgement. No advice. Just sit. It's ok to feel these things. We won't stay here long.

Furthermore, and really even more powerful, I know that my Savior understands the pain I am feeling. He too was isolated. He too must have felt deep cords of loneliness strike through his soul while on earth. He knows my pain, and he knows yours.

I also hold on to the promise from Scripture that I am not truly alone. I have a God who is called Immanuel which means "God is with us." I have a God who promises throughout Scripture that He is by my side. He is close to the broken-hearted with a special kind of closeness and comfort. I cling to that promise, even when it's difficult to feel.

I also know that many people truly do love me, and they're here for me. I am grateful for the bond we have through the family of God here on this earth, even though there is a very true reality to my feeling of loneliness right now. Especially in this new place. And, although I may be surrounded by loads of people, I am not truly known, and the loads of people can at times exasperate my feeling of loneliness.

Again, I am not expressing these things to seek attention. I am not expressing these feelings to find pity. I just know that God has called me to share life and truth through every season of my life, and this is my current season.

A season full of fear, but grounded in trust. A season full of loneliness, but grounded in fellowship with

Christ. A season full of feelings of loss, but grounded in the hope of expectation. A season full of brokenness, but grounded in comfort and healing through my loving God. A season full of weariness, but grounded in the rest I find through my compassionate Savior.

It's a tough one, but I know I'm not alone. I'm praying that if this finds you in a place of loneliness, isolation, or pain, that you will find fellowship in our brokenness. And most of all, that you will press in to God in the midst of the reality of your pain.

My number one piece of practical advice for you if you find yourself in a place of isolation is to reach out. *Just reach out.* So often we wait for someone else. And, many times, this is when the self-pity sets in. *Nobody cares about me. Nobody thinks of me. Nobody has a clue how hard my life is. And on and on it goes.* We can circle around and around on this planet of self-pity, or we can reach out. Be the first one to make a call to a friend. Don't wait for them to call or text you. Be the first one to introduce yourself. It might be out of your comfort zone, but what's the worst that could happen? Join a Bible Study. Lead a Bible Study. Find a Mom's Group. Find a Youth Group. Go volunteer. Invite a new acquaintance over for dinner. Do something to reach out. Do something to get your eyes off of yourself and onto someone else. And, you know what? You might just be relieving someone else from isolation, as well.

After Sam and I got married, I found myself in a very lonely place of isolation. I just hadn't found my place or people yet. So, I just started somewhere. I went to our church and asked if I could lead a Bible Study. I did, and I met women who became *my* people. My friends. My family. It took time, but as I poured into others, the feeling of isolation decreased and my joy increased.

What do you have to lose? Just reach out.

I'm in this with you.

DIVING DEEPER

Read:
Hebrews 10:22-25

As Christians, we can hold on to the promise that we are never alone. Discuss the fellowship available to every single believer in Christ.

_____

_____

_____

_____

PERSONAL REFLECTION

Have you neglected fellowship with God recently? If so, how and why?

_____

_____

_____

_____

Have you neglected fellowship with fellow believers lately? If so, how and why?

_____

_____

_____

_____

How will you enter into the presence of God this week?

_____
_____
_____
_____

How will you reach out to other believers this week?

_____
_____
_____
_____

CHALLENGE

Choose a fellow Christian to reach out to and "spur on toward love and good deeds."

Be sure to take part in some kind of gathering with fellow believers this week (church, small group, Bible study, a night of worship, etc)

DAY 6
Self-pity Extinguishes the Flame of Joy

I talked a little bit about self-pity in the last section, but I want to talk more about this extinguisher of joy. How do I know? Because I've thrown myself a fair share of pity parties!

Self-pity means, "excessive, self-absorbed unhappiness over one's own troubles." Could you possibly be living as one so self-involved that you are overly absorbed in your own personal troubles?

I found an article that explains self-pity in this way:
> When we indulge in self-pity, we have elevated our importance in our own eyes. Romans 12:3 says, "Do not think of yourself more highly than you ought." We are thinking too highly of ourselves when we allow life's hurts and injustices to dictate our emotional state. Bitterness can quickly override the fruit of the Holy Spirit (Galatians 5:22) that should be dominating the life of every believer. 1 Thessalonians 5:18–19 tells us that we are not to "quench the Holy Spirit." Instead, we are to give thanks in everything. It is impossible to give thanks while clinging to self-pity, because, by definition, a self-indulgent attitude is not focused on gratitude to others. Self-pity cannot be thankful at all for what God has allowed.

I love this explanation. Indulging in self-pity means

that our eyes are focused on self as central. As believers, we are to keep our eyes on Jesus, no matter the circumstances of life.

Furthermore, we are not to live in a state of defeat as followers of Christ. We are called to live in the victory of Jesus Christ. We are to live as *overcomers*, not as people *overcome* by the circumstances of life. We must move from *victim* to *victor*. Do you find yourself stuck in the victim-mentality? As Christians, we must shift from the victim-mentality to the victor-mentality.

In my upcoming book *The Struggle Is Real*, I explain how we operate as overcomers:

Only through the power of the Holy Spirit can we begin living for the Overcomer, the victorious One, who already defeated our Enemy. When we place our identity in the Overcomer, we too become overcomers! No longer overcome by the circumstances and trials of life. No longer overcome by the tactics of the Enemy. We are victorious, because Christ has made us victorious.

Stop living as one overcome. Step into your new identity, and live as an overcomer. It is time to move from victim to victor. From overcome to overcomer. *1 John 5:5 says: "Who is it that overcomes the world? Only the one who believes that Jesus is the Son of God."* In fact, "overcomer" is one of the final titles given to believers in the book of Revelation: *"All who overcome [are victorious] will become pillars in the Temple of God, and they will never have to leave it. And I will write my God's name on them, and they will be citizens in the city of my God – the new Jerusalem that comes down from heaven from my God. And they will have my new name inscribed upon them." (Revelation 3:12)*

In Christ, being an overcomer, a victorious one, is your new identity. Christians have been marked by God with

His name. Stop buying into the lies of who the Enemy says you are. Don't take on any name the Enemy may attempt to write on you. Mark yourself, define yourself, with the name of Jesus Christ. God sealed the victory 2,000 years ago by nailing the weight of our sin to the Cross. Jesus Christ, our Victor, made us alive through His death and resurrection. He became the Victorious One who transfers that victory to us. On the Cross, He disarmed the powers and authorities of this world and made a public spectacle of conquering the enemy, triumphing over them by the Cross. (Colossians 2:15)

Live in the power of that victory. Do not diminish the priceless sacrifice of Christ by giving in and living in self-pity as one defeated and overcome. Live as one alive and victorious. Boasting only in the Cross of Christ.

DIVING DEEPER
Read:
Romans 8:31-32

Self-pity causes us to live in a "woe is me" mentality. After reading Romans 8:31-32, why is this kind of mentality contrary to the way believers should live?

_____

_____

_____

_____

PERSONAL REFLECTION

Do you ever find yourself living with a victim mentality?

_____

_____

_____

_____

How do these verses encourage you to live in victory rather than living in defeat?

_____

_____

_____

_____

CHALLENGE

Write down 3 lies that are feeding your self-pity right now:

_____

_____

_____

Now, write down 3 truths from Scripture to counter those lies:

_____

_____

_____

DAY 7
Productivity + Purpose > Laziness + Misplaced Priorities

I can look back at every chapter of my life, and identify the times that I experienced the greatest delight and happiness. During each chapter, I have experienced seasons of joy. I also found myself in seasons of unsettled discontentment along the way. Looking back, I can clearly identify what facilitated the joy, and what facilitated the unsettledness. The joy overflowed from a place of living a productive and purposeful life. The unsettled, discontent spirit came during times of laziness and misplaced priorities. When I allowed myself to slip into a habit of laziness, I grew unsettled, discontentment, and just plain unhappy. When I chose the habit of productivity, I found myself living out my purpose as a follower of Christ.

This productivity looks different in the various chapters of your life. During high school, this meant choosing to disciple 3 younger girls before school each morning, rather than sleeping in a little later. In college it meant choosing to spend time studying the Bible, rather than binge watching Netflix. As a young married, this meant choosing to lead Bible Studies for women, rather than comparing myself to other young women. As a new mom, this meant choosing to shower, get dressed and choose rest with my little one, rather than sulk in self-pity in my quiet home. As a mom of a toddler, this means prioritizing my daughter and marriage, while continuing to write and minister to women, rather than complain about busy-ness and let myself waste my time.

Whatever chapter of life you're in, ask God how you can serve Him best. How can you use your specific gifting (because every single one of us has at least one spiritual gift) to further the Kingdom of God and bring glory to His name? Ask Him to reveal any laziness or misplaced priorities in your life and show you opportunities to replace that laziness with productivity for Kingdom Work!

I've been taught to ask God these 3 questions each day:
1. What do I need to stop doing?
2. What do I need to start doing?
3. What do I need to continue doing?

These are the perfect questions to keep yourself in check in this area.

A few very practical ways to get yourself into gear and rid yourself of laziness, because trust me, I could be a pro couch-potato if I let myself:
1. Instead of watching that TV show or instead of scrolling through your Instagram feed, open up your Bible. Grab your journal, and ask God to teach you something new today.
2. Self-focus is always a misplaced priority. Instead of focusing on yourself too much, look for an opportunity to pour into someone else today. Look for a chance to encourage someone else. Look for a chance to serve someone else. You'll be amazed at the affect an act of kindness can

have on someone else, and on yourself!
3. Just get dressed and lace up your tennis shoes. This may not apply to you in any way, but when I was a new mom, this was such a simple but sweet piece of advice I received. I was feeling low and a little purposeless, and an experienced mom told me to get dressed every day, lace up my shoes, and start the day. This simple piece of advice propelled me forward each day during that slow season of life.

And remember, purpose is not found in the big and grandiose. Purpose is found in the small and seemingly mundane. God uses the smallest, most mundane moments of life to create the richest, most meaningful interactions. Don't be surprised to find purpose in the most mundane circumstances of life.

DIVING DEEPER

Read:
Ecclesiastes 1:2-14

Why do you think Solomon (the writer of this passage) views everything in life as meaningless?

_____

_____

_____

_____

How can an eternal perspective & purpose in life, change this feeling of meaninglessness?

_____

_____

_____

PERSONAL REFLECTION

Do you ever find yourself viewing life like Solomon at times? If so, how and why?

_____

_____

_____

_____

Solomon looked back over his life only to find that nothing apart from God brought him happiness or joy. How can this realization from Solomon change the way you live your life?

_____

_____

_____

_____

CHALLENGE

Ask God these 3 questions:
1. What do I need to stop doing?
2. What do I need to start doing?
3. What do I need to continue doing?

_____

_____

_____

_____

Now stop, start, and continue whatever God tells you to do.

DAY 8
Unconfessed Sin = The Greatest Thief of Joy

Unconfessed sin. That lurking, dull ache in your gut. That indescribable, yet unmistakable barrier between you and the Father. When I have unconfessed sin lurking in my life, it's as if this unscalable brick wall has been built between my spirit and the Spirit of God, and that's the reason unconfessed sin is the greatest thief of joy. In the presence of God is where we find fullness of joy, and if that's true then when a barrier comes between our hearts and the heart of God, we lose our source of joy.

I remember a time in my life when I experienced this in an undeniable way. It might sound silly, but I had just had my first kiss. The problem was not with the kiss, but with the circumstances that surrounded the kiss. I had lied to my parents and told them I was going to a movie with friends. Instead, I met up with an older boy. No, a kiss is not sinful at all, but my deception was. I hid this from my parents for months. I remember going to church camp soon after all of this happened, still carrying the baggage of the unconfessed sin with me. As I tried to worship during the services, I felt numb. I couldn't get there. I couldn't connect with the heart of God. There was this wall. An emptiness ached in my soul. I missed the presence of God. Why couldn't I feel His presence? I realized that it was this unconfessed sin of lying to my parents that weighed on my heart. I knew I had to confess. Sadly, I never actually confessed…instead, my older brothers found out, terrorized the boy who had kissed me, and told my parents all about it. Although I was a little mad at my brothers, I was also relieved. When the hidden deception was out, it's as if this heavy weight was released. I found such relief in releasing the unconfessed sin I was carrying. And, most importantly, I was able to come before my Heavenly with my walls down and my heart open to His loving voice.

As a Girls' Minister, I found that many girls were walking around carrying different unconfessed sins that weighed on them without them even realizing it. It was difficult for them to pin-point the problem, but they just knew that didn't *feel* joy. They knew that they weren't experiencing or feeling the presence of God. They could decipher the feeling of a joyless spirit, but they couldn't decipher the source. As I sat down with girl after girl, talking through her different feelings, it often came back to the same thing…there was some kind of unconfessed sin in their lives.

Here's how some of those conversations would go…
Why do you feel such a heaviness? *Well, I'm not sure. I can't get this guilty feeling to go away.*
When did you start feeling the gnawing emptiness? *Probably after that party, when I got drunk.*
When did you stop feeling God's presence? *I think after my boyfriend and I starting getting way too physical.*
Do you think that mistake could be causing the barrier you're feeling between you and God? *I just didn't realize it was that big of a deal until now. I didn't know it would affect me as*

much as it has.

I could list conversation after conversation. Heavy heart after heavy heart. Dragging around the baggage of unconfessed sin. Unwilling to bring their mess before God. Sometimes unaware of the affect their sin was having on their spiritual life.

Unconfessed sin festers in our souls and eats away at our peace and joy. Confession unlocks the door to joy in our lives. Through confession, we allow the love, forgiveness, and acceptance of God to flood over our souls and plunge us into a place of incomprehensible, unexplainable joy.

Every time I talk with someone struggling with unconfessed sin, I encourage them to go read Psalm 51. I tell them to pray the same way David prayed in this Psalm. Each time I've suggested this, the person experiences an almost instantaneous joy. She finds joy by releasing the heavy burden of sin and coming before her loving Father just as she is. Stains and all. Because He is the Always-Forgiving, Miracle-Worker who is able to purify and create a renewed heart filled with joy.

DIVING DEEPER

Read:
Psalm 51

How did David view his sin? How does he describe how he feels about his sin?

_____

_____

_____

_____

What did David ask God to do with his sin?

_____

_____

_____

PERSONAL REFLECTION

Have you ever come before God in such godly sorrow over your sin? If so, when? And, what did you experience after?

_____

_____

_____

_____

Is it difficult for you to repent of your sins? Why or why not?

_____

_____

_____

_____

CHALLENGE

Ask God to reveal anything you need to repent of that may be causing a barrier between you and God.

Pray David's prayer as you bring yourself before God in repentance.

As you move forward...

As you move forward from here, I pray that each day you will sense God's presence and find yourself growing in the fullness of joy that only Jesus can provide.

Even after writing this 8-day challenge, I have to constantly revisit the principles in this devotional. I pray that this booklet will be the perfect gentle reminder when you need a reboot and refilling in the joy-department. Please do not get discouraged. Please do not give up.

When you feel defeated, come back to the filling station of God's grace, and allow Him to refill your soul when you feel depleted. We all become depleted. Life makes it difficult to constantly sustain a high-level of joy, but Jesus makes it possible. Continue to come before His presence and draw from the well of His endless riches. He will provide.

I'm praying over you, what I pray over my daughter constantly:

May the God of hope fill you with *all joy* and peace as you trust in Him, so that you may overflow with hope by the power of the Holy Spirit.

ABOUT THE AUTHOR

Tricia Patterson is a wife to Sam and a mom to a precious and beautiful daughter named Joy. She is a Bible teacher who is passionate about inspiring a younger generation to know Jesus in a personal way. Raised in a Christian home, Tricia accepted Christ at the age of 7, and she received a clear call into full-time ministry at the age of 14. Since that time, she has been teaching teenagers, groups of girls, and young women about her Savior.

Tricia graduated from Baylor University, Magna Cum Laude, with a Bachelor of Arts in Speech Communication. Later, she earned a Master of Arts degree in Christian Education with a concentration in Family Ministry from Dallas Baptist University.

Tricia's greatest joy in life is seeing others come from death to life, from darkness to light, through the saving work of Jesus Christ. She longs for others to find and experience the true life that only comes through Christ and Christ alone.

Website: www.TriciaPatterson.com
Connect with Tricia on a daily basis:
Blog: www.TriciaPatterson.com/blog
Instagram: @TLPat
Twitter: @TrishLPatterson

Made in the USA
Lexington, KY
28 September 2017